This journal

belongs to

_____

LIVE A PRAYING LIFE

Journal

JENNIFER KENNEDY DEAN

NEW HOPE
PUBLISHERS

Birmingham, Alabama

New Hope® Publishers
P. O. Box 12065
Birmingham, AL 35202-2065
www.newhopepublishers.com
New Hope Publishers is a division of WMU®.

Cover design: Left Coast Design, www.lcoast.com
Interior design: Sherry Hunt

ISBN-10: 1-59669-289-8
ISBN-13: 978-1-59669-289-3

N104146 • 0910 • 5M1

Quotations in this journal,
other than from the Bible,
are from these outstanding titles
by Jennifer Kennedy Dean:

Heart's Cry

The Life-Changing Power in the Name of Jesus

Life Unhindered!

Live a Praying Life

Pursuing the Christ

Secrets Jesus Shared

Set Apart

For more information, including news about upcoming titles,
and to purchase these or other books from New Hope Publishers
go to www.NewHopePublishers.com.

Introduction

*J*ournaling has been an important part of my own prayer journey, so I am pleased to invite you to join me in this discipline. A journal will become a record of your own history with God.

It can be an effective emotional outlet during times of stress or doubt. Journaling often helps me crystallize my thoughts and see them from a different perspective. It makes me grab hold of thoughts or emotions that hover on the edges, identify them, and give voice to them. It helps me track God's activity in my life and gives me a record of His faithfulness.

Experiment with different journaling methods and find your own rhythm. You don't have to journal the same way all the time. Let me suggest a few possible methods to get you started.

You might write out your thoughts as you express them to God. I often journal this way when I need to express confusion or doubt. It helps me pinpoint and define my exact sources of difficulty. I find that it gives me emotional release and also forces me to look at the direction of my thoughts. I also journal this way when I am praising Him and exulting in His faithfulness. Many of these outpourings of praise and adoration come from times when I have seen God work in ways that no one else would recognize because no one else has been in on our private conversations. If I had not recorded my exultation, I might even have forgotten these incidents.

Sometimes one anxious thought piles atop another without my stopping to deal with them until I am loaded down with anxieties I can't even name. David captures this well in Psalm 94:19 when he says, "When my anxious thoughts multiply within me" (NASB). I have a couple of ways that I journal my anxiety, and I find that it is eased and released as I do.

1. I write down something like: *These are the burdens I am trying to carry. As I write each down, I am laying it on Your altar. It is Yours now, not mine.* Then I list each anxiety or worry or fear. It is freeing because it is a concrete act. I find that as I list each anxiety separately, they don't look so bad. It is the piling of one on another that weighs me down. At the end I might write something like: *All Yours.* Or, *What You will, when You will, how You will.*

2. Another way that I sometimes deal with anxiety is to write out concrete statements of faith. Something like: *I know that nothing comes into my life without Your permission. I know that this situation is under Your control. I know that nothing is too difficult for You. I know that You are working in mighty ways right now in this situation.* As I write these kinds of statements, I know it is the Father reminding me of His promises and causing me to take hold of them.

Sometimes I write out my prayers. It focuses me. Sometimes I write out the Scripture that I sense the Lord has spoken to me. Sometimes I write out my questions to God, like: *What do You really mean by dying to self?* So I won't forget, I keep a record of seeming coincidences that turn out to be the micromanaging hand of God. Sometimes I pour out my heart like water in the presence of the Lord. Sometimes I write in code that only God and I would ever understand. Sometimes I just journal a word or a sentence.

Method doesn't matter. Just journal the journey. Let the daily thoughts and Scripture verses jump-start your conversation with the Father.

—Jennifer Kennedy Dean

Therefore if anyone is in Christ, there is a new creation;
old things have passed away, and look, new things have come.
—2 Corinthians 5:17 (HCSB)

I was made new when I accepted you as my Lord & Savior. I, at times, take the old man & put it back on me like a cloak w/ a hood. I have to remind myself DAILY to look to you and your mercies to fight the enemies arrows. Its your ways that will take me on the straight path not my own power. Show me, teach me, guide me. Help me to show up to & with you.

*N*ew, and then new again—that is Your gift to me today. A fresh slate, a new beginning, outrageous hope defined only by potential and possibility. —*Pursuing the Christ*

> *"You will seek me and find me when you seek me with all your heart. I will be found by you,"* declares the LORD.
> —Jeremiah 29:13–14

The key is seeking Him with my whole heart —
So often I ½ heartedly seek Him. I want to do my own thing. I want to have my way. When I "get" my way it is a disaster.
Teach me your ways O Lord that I might live long & prosper.

I f we seek Him, He will do the being found. He has made Himself easy to find. He is not hiding. He is pursuing us, wooing us, seeking us.
—*Life Unhindered!*

I look for blessings not
for Him often times.
Definitly not the right
approach —

"Nothing by any means
is going to hurt you!"

The eternal purpose —
and what a promise
it is !!

Therefore, I will not
fear !!

When He Himself is the focal point of our search—not blessings by way of Him, but *Him*—we are extravagantly, exorbitantly rewarded. When we find Him, we find everything. —*Live a Praying Life*

By Him everything was created, in heaven and on earth, the visible and the invisible, whether thrones or dominions or rulers or authorities — all things have been created through Him and for Him.
—Colossians 1:16 (HCSB)

Oh Lord this isn't a
foreign concept to me -
I believe it -
But I don't always
grasp the implications
of it -
I don't always live
like I get it

Time for Bible Study

*E*very cell and molecule, every atom, every neutrino, every particle of earth is of Your own design. You thought it and then formed it. You meticulously set each piece into place, ordering the universe perfectly.
—*Pursuing the Christ*

He does not take back his words.
—Isaiah 31:2

This is so ✗! Especially important for me as I age. Nothing can separate me from Him.

I have to trust "no matter what." The no matter what can include lots of things —

The Word of God, from beginning to end, tells us that God is sovereign and that He is working according to a plan that has been in place since before the earth was formed. Nothing takes Him by surprise. He is never making things up as He goes along. —*Live a Praying Life*

All this took place to fulfill what the Lord had said through the prophet: "The virgin will be with child and will give birth to a son, and they will call him Immanuel"—which means, "God with us."
—Matthew 1:22–23

Jesus, You are "God with us." I cannot quite grasp the fullness of it. Something more than God somewhere in the vicinity. More than God down the street. More than God within shouting distance. God *with* us.
—*Pursuing the Christ*

And pray in the Spirit on all occasions
with all kinds of prayers and requests.
—Ephesians 6:18

*P*rayer will work as God intends for it to work when it becomes what God intends for it to be. Prayer is not a formula, but a life. Only when we have learned to live prayer, breathe prayer, be prayer—only then will the power available through prayer be consistently manifested on the earth.
—*Live a Praying Life*

Pray without ceasing.
—1 Thessalonians 5:17 (NASB)

*P*rayer is not an activity, but a relationship. Prayer is a relationship more intimate than any you can know with another person, because in prayer you draw on the life of Christ within you. —*Heart's Cry*

Before a word is on my tongue
you know it completely, O Lord.
—Psalm 139:4

Before a need or desire has reached a level of conscious under-standing at which you can put it into words—while it is still unformed and raw—God already knows it fully. —*Live a Praying Life*

"If you had responded to my rebuke, I would have poured out my heart to you and made my thoughts known to you."
—Proverbs 1:23

The Potter is shaping your heart so that it is the container for His desires. He is creating a masterpiece of His own design. He is forming a vessel into which He will pour out His heart. —*Live a Praying Life*

*"I will remove from you your heart of stone
and give you a heart of flesh."*
—Ezekiel 36:26

he original law was engraved on stone tablets by the finger of God.
When a stone is engraved, the markings are cut into the stone and
become one with it. When God engraves His law on your heart, His law
becomes one with your heart. Your heart changes. —*Set Apart*

One day Jesus was praying in a certain place.
When he finished, one of his disciples said to him,
"Lord, teach us to pray, just as John taught his disciples."
—Luke 11:1

_____

_____

_____

_____

_____

_____

_____

_____

_____

_____

_____

_____

_____

_____

_____

_____

*P*rayer is more than the words you say that come sandwiched between "Dear God" and "Amen." Prayer is an openness to and awareness of His presence and His power in your life. —*Secrets Jesus Shared*

The Spirit himself intercedes for us with groans that words cannot express. And he who searches our hearts knows the mind of the Spirit, because the Spirit intercedes for the saints in accordance with God's will.
—Romans 8:26–27

When a desire is nothing but an inarticulate groan—before you can form it into sentences—the Spirit of God is already speaking it with perfect clarity. —*Live a Praying Life*

O Lord Almighty, you who examine the righteous
and probe the heart and mind.
—Jeremiah 20:12

_____

_____

_____

_____

_____

_____

_____

_____

_____

_____

_____

_____

_____

_____

_____

_____

_____

_____

God understands the things about you that you do not understand about yourself. He knows you like no one else knows you, and He loves you at a depth you cannot fathom. —*The Life-Changing Power in the Name of Jesus*

May your unfailing love be my comfort,
according to your promise to your servant.
Let your compassion come to me that I may live,
for your law is my delight.
—Psalm 119:76–77

As you are learning to live a praying life, prayer takes on a much broader definition than "saying prayers." Many times the direct answers to petitions are the least important aspect of what the prayer accomplished. As you progress and mature into a praying life, your testimony of prayer's effectiveness will be that the mercies of God unfold at every turn. —*Live a Praying Life*

And my God will meet all your needs
according to his glorious riches in Christ Jesus.
—Philippians 4:19

Father, thank You for my needs because they lead me to Your supply.
Glorify Yourself through my needs. —*Heart's Cry*

Indeed, we have all received grace after grace from His fullness,
for although the law was given through Moses,
grace and truth came through Jesus Christ.
—John 1:16–17 (HCSB)

orn again into Your bloodline, grace flows to me, through me, and from me. —*Pursuing the Christ*

"Here I am! I stand at the door and knock.
If anyone hears my voice and opens the door,
I will come in and eat with him, and he with me."
—Revelation 3:20

God initiates prayer. The Scripture tells us that God is awakening desires, initiating spiritual hunger, creating in His children the inclination to seek Him. —*Live a Praying Life*

"I have put my words in your mouth
and covered you with the shadow of my hand."
—Isaiah 51:16

_____

_____

_____

_____

_____

_____

_____

_____

_____

_____

_____

_____

_____

_____

_____

_____

_____

_____

_____

True prayer is when God's heart is expressed through your words. Prayer in its highest form occurs when the words I articulate, with my mouth or in my mind, are merely the containers for God's thoughts and desires. —*Live a Praying Life*

*But whatever was to my profit I now consider loss
for the sake of Christ. What is more, I consider everything
a loss compared to the surpassing greatness of knowing
Christ Jesus my Lord, for whose sake I have lost all things.
I consider them rubbish, that I may gain Christ.*
—Philippians 3:7–8

The praying life is a life of diligence. In the praying life, we welcome
Him as the Refiner's Fire, burning away every distraction.
—*Live a Praying Life*

"'Take the talent from him and give it to the one who has the ten talents. For everyone who has will be given more, and he will have an abundance. Whoever does not have, even what he has will be taken from him. And throw that worthless servant outside, into the darkness, where there will be weeping and gnashing of teeth.'"
—Matthew 25:28–30

If we want to live in the fullness of the kingdom, we have to put ourselves at risk. The mistake that the servant with one talent made was that he feared losing what he had and, thus, lost the opportunity to gain more. —*Secrets Jesus Shared*

"Blessed are those who hunger and thirst for righteousness, for they will be filled."
—Matthew 5:6

Jesus is filling us with Himself, and with His righteousness. —*Set Apart*

If we are faithless, he will remain faithful,
for he cannot disown himself.
—2 Timothy 2:13

Will Jesus remove His love from you because of disobedience? No! Nothing can separate you from the love of God. He has settled His love on you. —*Live a Praying Life*

"The LORD your God carried you as a man carries his son."
—Deuteronomy 1:31 (HCSB)

Eternal Father, I yield myself to Your tender care.
—*Pursuing the Christ*

Show me your face, let me hear your voice; for your voice is sweet, and your face is lovely.
—Song of Songs 2:14

How tenderly You call my name, offering eternity; drawing me ever deeper into Your great heart. Like a magnet, Your irresistible pull is unrelenting. I surrender to Your gentle wooing, at last to find that You are my heart's cry. —*Heart's Cry*

"Do not be afraid, little flock,
for your Father has been pleased to give you the kingdom."
—Luke 12:32

His heart is set on you to do you good. —*Live a Praying Life*

Perfect love drives out fear.
—1 John 4:18

----

*G*od is perfect love. Fear cannot exist in His presence. —*Heart's Cry*

We demolish arguments and every pretension that sets itself up against the knowledge of God, and we take captive every thought to make it obedient to Christ.
—2 Corinthians 10:5

*P*rayer is the most aggressive, offensive, proactive, invasive work you can ever engage in. We're not talking here about just "saying prayers." This is *living prayer.* —*Live a Praying Life*

Arise, cry out in the night, as the watches of the night begin;
pour out your heart like water in the presence of the Lord.
—Lamentations 2:19

_____

_____

_____

_____

_____

_____

_____

_____

_____

_____

_____

_____

_____

_____

_____

_____

_____

_____

_____

_____

God is always listening for your cry. —*Heart's Cry*

Delight yourself in the LORD
and he will give you the desires of your heart.
—Psalm 37:4

D uring the process of prayer, this truth takes on its richest, deepest meaning. You find that when you delight yourself in the Lord, He *becomes* the desire of your heart. —*Live a Praying Life*

"And everyone who has left houses or brothers or sisters or father or mother or children or fields for my sake will receive a hundred times as much and will inherit eternal life."
—Matthew 19:29

When the benefit far outweighs the cost, we call it gain. Disciple-ship will cost you everything you have, but it will gain you even more. —*Secrets Jesus Shared*

"Today, if you hear his voice, do not harden your hearts."
—Hebrews 4:7

*F*ollow Me. Live My life in your world. Express My love. Speak My words. You are My chosen instrument. You are living proof that I Am.
—*Heart's Cry*

"On this rock I will build my church, and the gates of Hades will not overcome it. I will give you the keys of the kingdom of heaven; whatever you bind on earth will be bound in heaven, and whatever you loose on earth will be loosed in heaven."
—Matthew 16:18–19

The church is God's expression of Himself in the world. The church is the physical presence of Christ on earth. —*Heart's Cry*

I cry out to God Most High, to God,
who fulfills his purpose for me.
—Psalm 57:2

We seek God through the spiritual disciplines. By engaging in the spiritual disciplines, we keep our lives open to God so that He can do in us and through us what He desires. —*Live a Praying Life*

*"I looked for a man among them who would build up the wall
and stand before me in the gap on behalf of the land
so I would not have to destroy it, but I found none."*
—Ezekiel 22:30

_W_hat God wants to do on the earth, He will do through intercessors. When God wants to change the course events will take on their own, He calls out an intercessor. —*Live a Praying Life*

For we are to God the aroma of Christ.
—2 Corinthians 2:15

We are living prayers. Our lives are the aroma of Christ rising before God continually as a sweet-smelling offering. —*Heart's Cry*

So we fix our eyes not on what is seen, but on what is unseen.
For what is seen is temporary, but what is unseen is eternal.
—2 Corinthians 4:18

*P*rayer is the means by which you will be freed from your earthbound, timebound thinking to participate in eternity. —*Live a Praying Life*

"Your kingdom come,
your will be done on earth as it is in heaven."
—Matthew 6:10

His sovereign decree has established prayer as the bridge between the spiritual world—where His Word is settled forever and where all the promises of God are already "Yes" in Christ—and the material world. Prayer bridges the gap between heaven and earth.
—*Live a Praying Life*

The prayer of a righteous man is powerful and effective.
—James 5:16

---

*P*rayer changes the earth. The spiritual power that prayer releases has authority over the earth. The earth is subject to the power of the Spirit. —*Live a Praying Life*

*"The Holy Spirit will come upon you, and the power of the
Most High will overshadow you. Therefore the holy
One to be born will be called the Son of God....
For nothing will be impossible with God."*
—Luke 1:35, 37 (HCSB)

You never promise anything that You do not have all the power
necessary to accomplish. —*Pursuing the Christ*

The path of the righteous is like the first gleam of dawn,
shining ever brighter till the full light of day.
—Proverbs 4:18

God reveals His will progressively. He unfolds it obedience by obedience. —*Set Apart*

Devote yourselves to prayer, being watchful and thankful.
—Colossians 4:2

Always be alert to the Holy Spirit's leadership in prayer. Through Him, be alert to the blessings of God that call you to thanksgiving.
—Heart's Cry

*For no matter how many promises God has made,
they are "Yes" in Christ.*
—2 Corinthians 1:20

_____

_____

_____

_____

_____

_____

_____

_____

_____

_____

_____

_____

_____

_____

_____

_____

_____

_____

G od doesn't make empty promises or write bad checks. Jesus is the
reality that stands behind every promise God has ever made.
—*Life Unhindered!*

For the mind-set of the flesh is death,
but the mind-set of the Spirit is life and peace.
—Romans 8:6 (HCSB)

*I*ncarnate Word, You came to set my captive thoughts free and to captivate my restless mind and anchor it in You. —*Pursuing the Christ*

This is love: not that we loved him, but that he loved us....
We love because He first loved us.
—1 John 4:10,19

_____

_____

_____

_____

_____

_____

_____

_____

_____

_____

_____

_____

_____

_____

_____

_____

_____

_____

*I*t is His pull on our hearts that causes us to desire Him. Without His initiative, we would never seek Him out. When we find within ourselves the initiative to seek God, it is really a response to His invitation to seek Him. —*Live a Praying Life*

For the wages of sin is death.
—Romans 6:23

When sin pays you what you've earned, you get death. Jesus took upon Himself what you and I have earned and deserve. —*Set Apart*

It is for freedom that Christ has set us free.
—Galatians 5:1

True freedom is provided by Christ, and apart from Him no one can be truly free. —*Life Unhindered!*

But he was pierced for our transgressions, he was crushed for our iniquities; the punishment that brought us peace was upon him, and by his wounds we are healed. We all, like sheep, have gone astray, each of us has turned to his own way; and the LORD has laid on him the iniquity of us all.
—Isaiah 53:5–6

God does not ignore or pass over our sins. He has punished them fully and completely. When Jesus died His unimaginably savage, bloody, brutal death the punishment for all our sins was being enacted upon His body. —*The Life-Changing Power in the Name of Jesus*

"Quick! Bring the best robe and put it on him."
—Luke 15:22

*W*ho owned the best robe? The father did. The father called for *his own robe* to cover the son's shame and failure.
—*Secrets Jesus Shared*

He does not treat us as our sins deserve
or repay us according to our iniquities.
—Psalm 103:10

Mercy always has redemption as its goal. What will redeem and restore and heal? That is the course mercy will take. —*Set Apart*

The mystery of godliness is great:
He was manifested in the flesh.
—1 Timothy 3:16 (HCSB)

---

he purpose for Your birth was Your death. The purpose for Your death was Your resurrection. The purpose for Your resurrection was my salvation. —*Pursuing the Christ*

*"He will be like a tree planted by the water
that sends out its roots by the stream."*
—Jeremiah 17:8

The Lord wants to make your life like a watered garden. He wants your life to be lush with the Spirit's fruit. —*Live a Praying Life*

Godly sorrow brings repentance that leads to salvation and leaves no regret, but worldly sorrow brings death.
—2 Corinthians 7:10

_____

_____

_____

_____

_____

_____

_____

_____

_____

_____

_____

_____

_____

_____

_____

_____

_____

_____

_____

*J*esus' sorrow over your sin, transfused into your heart, results in repentance. Repentance leads to salvation—not just the initial acceptance of eternal salvation, but continual salvation from the sins that have a grip on you. —*Set Apart*

God has given us eternal life, and this life is in his Son.
He who has the Son has life; he who does not have the
Son of God does not have life.
—1 John 5:11–12

Eternal life is far more than an addendum to our life when we die. Eternal life is a new kind of life that we receive the very moment we receive the Son. This eternal, abundant, overflowing life is in Jesus, and Jesus is in us. —*Secrets Jesus Shared*

A better covenant,
which was established upon better promises.
—Hebrews 8:6 (KJV)

*I*n the New Covenant, God Himself speaks to each of His children from inside, through His indwelling presence. —*Live a Praying Life*

God's love was revealed among us in this way: God sent His One and Only Son into the world so that we might live through Him. Love consists in this: not that we loved God, but that He loved us and sent His Son to be the propitiation for our sins.
—1 John 4:9–10 (HCSB)

_____

_____

_____

_____

_____

_____

_____

_____

_____

_____

_____

_____

_____

_____

_____

_____

_____

_____

Knowing that You have given *to me* Your finest treasure, I can rest assured that You will not withhold anything good from me.
—*Pursuing the Christ*

"And do not set your heart on what you will eat or drink;
do not worry about it. For the pagan world runs after all such
things, and your Father knows that you need them. But seek
his kingdom, and these things will be given to you as well."
—Luke 12:29–31

The kingdom is invisible, yet those who have entered the kingdom will see its effects in the material realm. Jesus tells His disciples that when they seek the kingdom, all the things they need will be added to them as well. —*Secrets Jesus Shared*

May I never boast except in the cross of our Lord Jesus Christ,
through which the world has been crucified to me,
and I to the world.
—Galatians 6:14

The only thing that belongs to us and to which we can cling is the Cross of our Lord Jesus Christ. In order to cling to the power of that Cross, we have to let go of everything else. —*Life Unhindered!*

Let us draw near to God with a sincere heart in full assurance of faith, having our hearts sprinkled to cleanse us from a guilty conscience and having our bodies washed with pure water.
—Hebrews 10:22

A clean heart, or a pure, unadulterated heart, is a requirement for mountain-moving prayer. —*Heart's Cry*

And the blood of Jesus, his Son, purifies us from all sin.
—1 John 1:7

You are continuously being cleansed of all unrighteousness because He lives His life through you. His life is always flowing through you, flushing away impurities. *—Heart's Cry*

"Every branch that does bear fruit
he prunes so that it will be even more fruitful."
—John 15:2–3

G od is a pruner. He cuts away foliage that looks beautiful, but is instead a life-drain. Sometimes the things we get most attached to, the things we are most proud of, are only taking up space where lasting fruit could be growing. —*Life Unhindered!*

"Which of you, if his son asks for bread, will give him a stone? Or if he asks for a fish, will give him a snake? If you, then, though you are evil, know how to give good gifts to your children, how much more will your Father in heaven give good gifts to those who ask him!"
—Matthew 7:9–11

Often, in order to give you the desire of your heart, God will withhold the desire of the moment. He only says no as a prelude to a higher yes. Give Him time—give Him access—so that He can peel back the desire of the moment and show you the desire of your heart. To the desire of your heart, there will always be a resounding yes from heaven.
—*Live a Praying Life*

"If you remain in me and my words remain in you, ask whatever you wish, and it will be given you."
—John 15:7

The person who is abiding in Christ has desires that are God-shaped. Out of the life that is abandoned to God and His purposes flows the prayer that God has promised to answer. —*Live a Praying Life*

"It is God who works in you to will and to act according to his good purpose."
—Philippians 2:13

He works *in* you, not just on you, or for you, or with you. In you. His power working in you is recreating your desires so that they match His. —*Life Unhindered!*

*"Do not store up for yourselves treasures on earth,
where moth and rust destroy, and where thieves break in and steal.
But store up for yourselves treasures in heaven, where moth and
rust do not destroy, and where thieves do not break in and steal.
For where your treasure is, there your heart will be also."*
—Matthew 6:19–21

If you consider your treasure to be on earth, then that is where you heart will be focused. If you consider your treasure to be in the spiritual realm, then that is where you heart will be focused.
—*Secrets Jesus Shared*

I wait for the LORD, my soul waits,
and in his word I put my hope.
—Psalm 130:5

God has good, loving, and productive reasons for scheduling waiting periods into the prayer process. When He has called on you to wait, it is because what He is doing during the waiting time is necessary for the best outcome. —*Live a Praying Life*

"I tell you the truth, unless a kernel of wheat falls to the ground and dies, it remains only a single seed. But if it dies, it produces many seeds."
—John 12:24

Where is the life in a seed? It's in the seed's embryo, which contains the blueprint for life. The husk, the tough outer layer that encases the seed, must be broken down so water and oxygen can reach the embryo, the life center. The outer layer must die so the life contained within the seed can emerge. —*Secrets Jesus Shared*

*All the ways of the Lord are loving and faithful
to those who keep the demands of his covenant.*
—Psalm 25:10

*F*aith is not knowing *how* God will bring His will into being; faith is knowing *that* God will bring His will into being. —*Live a Praying Life*

*The LORD caused the men throughout the camp
to turn on each other with their swords.*
—Judges 7:22

It was not the ingenious battle plan that gave Gideon the victory. It was the faith to obey the voice of *Jehovah Shalom.*
—*The Life-Changing Power in the Name of Jesus*

As you do not know the path of the wind, or how the body is formed in a mother's womb, so you cannot understand the work of God, the Maker of all things.
—Ecclesiastes 11:5

_____

_____

_____

_____

_____

_____

_____

_____

_____

_____

_____

_____

_____

_____

_____

_____

When you treat prayer as if you have the right to tell God how to do His work, you will be disappointed. God does not take instructions.
—*Live a Praying Life*

By faith Abraham, when he was called, obeyed.
—Hebrews 11:8 (NASB)

here did Abraham's faith begin? With God's call. How was it manifested? In Abraham's obedience. —*Heart's Cry*

So we fix our eyes not on what is seen, but on what is unseen.
For what is seen is temporary, but what is unseen is eternal.
—2 Corinthians 4:18

God is the big picture. When He is the focal point, then everything else takes on the proper dimensions. We see things in perspective. Big God. Little circumstances. —*Life Unhindered!*

"For my thoughts are not your thoughts, neither are your ways my ways," declares the LORD. "As the heavens are higher than the earth, so are my ways higher than your ways and my thoughts than your thoughts."
—Isaiah 55:8–9

He does not have one-size-fits-all answers. God's agenda is always bigger than the immediate circumstances. —*Live a Praying Life*

Now if any of you lacks wisdom, he should ask God,
who gives to all generously and without criticizing,
and it will be given to him.
—James 1:5 (HCSB)

I lay before You now . . . everything this day holds. I ask now for Your wisdom, Wonderful Counselor. —*Pursuing the Christ*

Now to him who is able to do immeasurably more than all we ask or imagine, according to his power that is at work within us.
—Ephesians 3:20

Are you trying to hold God to the best thing you can think of? Right now, would you tell God that you are aligning yourself with the best thing He can think of? —*Live a Praying Life*

"Give us today our daily bread."
—Matthew 6:11

The Father wants to meet your needs. He encourages you to look to Him to supply every need that arises. He takes pleasure in supplying you with everything you need. —*Set Apart*

Let us run with perseverance
the race marked out for us.
—Hebrews 12:1

Our race is a long-distance run. There is no quick-fix, microwaveable version. Faith, patience, endurance, and stamina are required. The kind of power that enables perseverance is exactly the kind of power Jesus has available. —*Life Unhindered!*

Consider it pure joy, my brothers, whenever you face trials of many kinds, because you know that the testing of your faith develops perseverance. Perseverance must finish its work so that you may be mature and complete, not lacking anything.
—James 1:2–4

*P*erseverance brings something valuable and solid into our lives. It's not just perseverance for the sake of perseverance, but perseverance as the doorway to something more. *—Life Unhindered!*

And immediately the boat reached the shore where they were heading.
—John 6:21

What the disciples would someday learn is that the *presence* of Jesus is the *destination.* —*The Life-Changing Power in the Name of Jesus*

"Be still, and know that I am God."
—Psalm 46:10

The Spirit's quiet whisper
Bids me bow before Your throne
'Til my heart's deepest yearnings
Are the echo of Your own.
—*Live a Praying Life*

"Therefore I am now going to allure her;
I will lead her into the desert and speak tenderly to her."
—Hosea 2:14

To seek God, we must build into our lives the discipline of solitude and silence. We must respond when the Father calls us to a place of solitude to be alone with Him. —*Live a Praying Life*

The fruit of righteousness will be peace;
the effect of righteousness will be quietness and confidence forever.
—Isaiah 32:17

_____

_____

_____

_____

_____

_____

_____

_____

_____

_____

_____

_____

_____

_____

_____

_____

_____

Apple trees grow apples. Peach trees grow peaches. You can identify a tree by its fruit. What is the fruit of righteousness? Peace.
—*Set Apart*

"Blessed are the peacemakers,
for they will be called sons of God."
—Matthew 5:9

_A_ strong, settled, contented person, anchored to eternity's realities, has the courage and the boldness to be outrageous in making peace. —*Set Apart*

Let us, therefore, make every effort to enter that rest.
—Hebrews 4:11

There is a walk of discipline and integrity that leads to rest. It starts with choosing to cooperate with the Spirit and deliberately relinquishing your own best ideas and efforts to His indwelling power. —*Life Unhindered!*

You will be like a well-watered garden.
—Isaiah 58:11

_W_eed out bitterness. Let praise take root and flourish. Cultivate my life so that it will display Your beauty. Make my life like a watered garden, lush with the Spirit's fruit. *—Heart's Cry*

"Still other seed fell on good soil.
It came up, grew and produced a crop,
multiplying thirty, sixty, or even a hundred times."
—Mark 4:8

_I_ am captured by the idea of the 100-fold increase. If there is a 100-fold increase to be had, then I want it. —*Secrets Jesus Shared*

Who may ascend the hill of the LORD?
Who may stand in his holy place?
He who has clean hands and a pure heart.
—Psalm 24:3–4

*P*ower flows from purity. Seek purity and you will find power.
—*Live a Praying Life*

But just as he who called you is holy, so be holy in all you do;
for it is written: "Be holy, because I am holy."
—1 Peter 1:15–16

*B*lessed means the quality of life that God Himself possesses. You were created to live in a state of blessedness, and it is established through holiness. —*Set Apart*

What I have forgiven—if there was anything to forgive—
I have forgiven in the sight of Christ for your sake,
in order that Satan might not outwit us.
For we are not unaware of his schemes.
—2 Corinthians 2:10–11

As you forgive those who have wronged you, you close the door to
Satan's schemes and you open the door to the power of God.
—*Secrets Jesus Shared*

By faith Abraham, when called to go to a place
he would later receive as his inheritance, obeyed and went,
even though he did not know where he was going.
—Hebrews 11:8

aith is not believing *something*. Faith is believing *Someone*. Faith is not committing yourself to an idea, but to a Person. Faith is responding to the present-tense voice of the Father. —*Live a Praying Life*

O Lord, our Lord,
how majestic is your name in all the earth!
—Psalm 8:9

A mere word cannot convey who God is, but as we encounter Him in personal ways and experience Him in action, we begin to know His name. —*The Life-Changing Power in the Name of Jesus*

"She will give birth to a son, and you are to give him the name Jesus, because he will save his people from their sins."
—Matthew 1:21

W ho named Jesus? His Father named Him. His Father named the Son after Himself: Jesus means "Jehovah Saves."
—The Life-Changing Power in the Name of Jesus

He will be named . . . Mighty God.
—Isaiah 9:6 (HCSB)

Jesus, let me know You as Mighty God. Speak into my heart and mind and soul that You are Mighty God and all power is in Your hand.
—*Pursuing the Christ*

They exchanged the truth of God for a lie.
—Romans 1:25

Where the truth belongs, a lie stands instead. That is our natural state. When we encounter and accept Christ, He begins to progressively replace lies with truth. It's all about lies and truth. *—Life Unhindered!*

The people walking in darkness have seen a great light;
on those living in the land of darkness, a light has dawned.
—Isaiah 9:2 (HCSB)

ntil I saw You, I had never seen light. Until my heart found that light it craved, I was living in darkness and in the shadow of death. Bring Your light into every corner of my life. —*Pursuing the Christ*

When Jesus spoke again to the people, he said,
"I am the light of the world. Whoever follows me
will never walk in darkness, but will have the light of life."
—John 8:12

Darkness comes in two forms. One is the absence of light. The other is blindness. Jesus is the Light that overcomes both.
—The Life-Changing Power in the Name of Jesus

He humbled himself and became obedient to death—even death on a cross! Therefore God exalted him to the highest place and gave him the name that is above every name.
—Philippians 2:8–9

We are fixing our gaze on Jesus, who stripped down and ran the bruising course that won our salvation. He ran with determination—single-minded in His pursuit, tenacious in His resolve. When He hit the wall, He powered through. He ran to win, and He won the prize.
—*Life Unhindered!*

But we have this treasure in jars of clay to show that this all-surpassing power is from God and not from us.
—2 Corinthians 4:7

He has decided to condition the release of His power on the prayers of His children. Because His power is all-sufficient, because it needs nothing to help it out or add to it, He can demonstrate His power even through jars of clay. *—Live a Praying Life*

On my bed I remember you;
I think of you through the watches of the night.
—Psalm 63:6

*I*nstead of thinking on the pressures tomorrow holds, or the stresses of the day just ending, center your thoughts on God. Let thoughts of Him fill your mind. —*Heart's Cry*

Anyone who lives on milk, being still an infant,
is not acquainted with the teaching about righteousness.
But solid food is for the mature, who by constant use
have trained themselves to distinguish good from evil.
—Hebrews 5:13–14

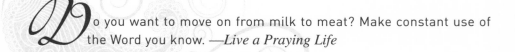

Do you want to move on from milk to meat? Make constant use of the Word you know. *—Live a Praying Life*

But his delight is in the law of the LORD,
and on his law he meditates day and night.
—Psalm 1:2

You ou can delight in the Lord by meditating on His Word.
—*Heart's Cry*

"If you remain in me and my words remain in you,
ask whatever you wish, and it will be given you."
—John 15:7

As you make your heart's home in His Word, you will find your desires initiated and guided by Him. —*Heart's Cry*

The meditation of my heart will be understanding.
—Psalm 49:3 (NASB)

----

*M*editation is focused listening. It is coming before God, expecting Him to unfold His Word to you. —*Heart's Cry*

And we, who with unveiled faces all reflect the Lord's glory,
are being transformed into his likeness with ever-increasing glory,
which comes from the Lord, who is the Spirit.
—2 Corinthians 3:18

_____

_____

_____

_____

_____

_____

_____

_____

_____

_____

_____

_____

_____

_____

_____

_____

_____

_____

_____

The promise of prayer is a transformed heart. Through the ongoing discipline of prayer, we are brought into direct and intimate contact with the Father's heart. As we continually behold His glory, we are changed into His image. Our lives begin to reflect Him; our desires begin to reflect His desires. —*Live a Praying Life*

Now to him who is able to do immeasurably more than all we ask or imagine, according to his power that is at work within us.
—Ephesians 3:20–21

Dear friend, put away childish things—little flesh-shaped desires; shortsighted, earthbound understanding. Yield yourself to His bigger agenda. Let Him do more than you can ask or even think.
—*Live a Praying Life*

Whatever was to my profit
I now consider loss for the sake of Christ.
—Philippians 3:7

---

*I*n His presence, I am changed. In the light of His presence, circumstances may stay the same, but my interpretation is revolutionized.
—*Heart's Cry*

"Who can tip over the water jars of the heavens when the dust becomes hard and the clods of earth stick together?"
—Job 38:37–38

he same One who pours out rain on the earth to soften the hardened soil can pour out the Holy Spirit on your heart right where it is least penetrable and most resistant. —*Secrets Jesus Shared*

"Break up your unplowed ground."
—Jeremiah 4:3

When the Lord is turning over the soil in your heart, don't try to pat it all back down and make it nice and even like it used to be. Let the Lord prepare the ground for the seed He wants to plant there.
—*Secrets Jesus Shared*

The LORD *confides in those who fear him;*
he makes his covenant known to them.
—Psalm 25:14

G od's heart is the beginning point of prayer. Powerful, earth-changing prayer begins in the heart of God and flows through the hearts of His people. —*Live a Praying Life*

We always carry around in our body the death of Jesus,
so that the life of Jesus may also be revealed in our body.
—2 Corinthians 4:10

The power of His death works *in* you, so the power of His life can work *through* you. —*Life Unhindered!*

A man reaps what he sows.
—Galatians 6:7

When you harvest the promises of God in your life, each promise has the seed of more promise in it. It is a principle of growth in the kingdom. —*Secrets Jesus Shared*

*"As the Father has loved me, so have I loved you.
Now remain in my love. If you obey my commands,
you will remain in my love, just as I have obeyed my Father's
commands and remain in his love. I have told you this so that my
joy may be in you and that your joy may be complete."*
—John 15:9–11

Obedience by obedience, my heart softens and I become more astute
at hearing His voice. —*Live a Praying Life*

"This is my Son, whom I love. Listen to him!"
—Mark 9:7

_____
_____
_____
_____
_____
_____
_____
_____
_____
_____
_____
_____
_____
_____
_____
_____

The clutter in our hearts throws off its acoustics. *Acoustics* are defined as "the qualities that determine the ability of an enclosure to reflect sound waves in such a way as to produce distinct hearing." How are your heart's acoustics? Does God need to do some renovation?
—*Live a Praying Life*

"*My soul proclaims the greatness of the Lord,
and my spirit has rejoiced in God my Savior,
because He has looked with favor
on the humble condition of His slave.*"
—Luke 1:46–48 (HCSB)

I want my soul—all that I am—I want my soul to proclaim Your greatness. —*Pursuing the Christ*

In the beginning was the Word, and the Word was with God,
and the Word was God. He was with God in the beginning.
Through him all things were made; without him nothing was
made that has been made. In him was life,
and that life was the light of men.
—John 1:1–4

The Word Who was from the beginning is the living and present Jesus, Who has taken up residence in you and in me as His followers, making us His home. —*Set Apart*

When your words came, I ate them;
they were my joy and my heart's delight.
—Jeremiah 15:16

The Word of God nourishes your spirit just as food nourishes your body.
—*Heart's Cry*

"My burden is light."
—Matthew 11:30

Other rabbis made the Law heavier and heavier, more and more burdensome. Rabbi Jesus said that His yoke is easy and His burden light. —*Secrets Jesus Shared*

"If anyone is thirsty, let him come to me and drink. Whoever believes in me, as the Scripture has said, streams of living water will flow from within him."
—John 7:37–38

Living water in, living water out. What Jesus pours into us, He pours out through us. The Holy Spirit, the Spirit of Christ in us, is the living water. —*Life Unhindered!*

We have not received the spirit of the world but the Spirit who is from God, that we may understand what God has freely given us.
—1 Corinthians 2:12

He has given us His Spirit. He has given us Himself. The purpose for giving us His Spirit is so that we can understand what He has prepared for us and has made freely available to us.
—*Live a Praying Life*

For you died,
and your life is now hidden with Christ in God.
—Colossians 3:3

He poured out His life *for* us so that He could pour out His life *in* us.
—*The Life-Changing Power in the Name of Jesus*

When he saw the crowds, he had compassion on them, because they were harassed and helpless, like sheep without a shepherd. Then he said to his disciples, "The harvest is plentiful but the workers are few. Ask the Lord of the harvest, therefore, to send out workers into his harvest field."

—Matthew 9:36–38

When Jesus is reproducing His heart in you, His compassion and sorrow for those who are lost and going their own way will spill over into your heart. —*Set Apart*

"For we have no power to face this vast army that is attacking us.
We do not know what to do, but our eyes are upon you."
—2 Chronicles 20:12

*T*his should be the attitude of any fast. In disengaging ourselves from our physical world for a time, we fasten our attention on God.
—Heart's Cry

"But when you fast, put oil on your head and wash your face, so that it will not be obvious to men that you are fasting, but only to your Father, who is unseen; and your Father, who sees what is done in secret, will reward you."
—Matthew 6:17–18

asting will sensitize you to the things of the spiritual realm so that you will be more aware of His presence and His present-tense voice. What is God's reward? Himself. —*Live a Praying Life*

"Is not this the kind of fasting I have chosen: to loose the chains of injustice and untie the cords of the yoke, to set the oppressed free and break every yoke? Is it not to share your food with the hungry and to provide the poor wanderer with shelter—when you see the naked, to clothe him, and not to turn away from your own flesh and blood?"
—Isaiah 58:6–7

When fasting is Spirit-led, it gives God access to you. It breaks down barriers that might have been erected. It increases your receptivity to Him. The result of fasting will show up in your living. —*Heart's Cry*

Pray in the Spirit on all occasions
with all kinds of prayers and requests.
—Ephesians 6:18

*I*t is through the Holy Spirit that the life of Christ is operative within you. True prayer cannot happen apart from the Spirit of God.
—*Heart's Cry*

The weapons we fight with are not the weapons of the world.
On the contrary, they have divine power to demolish strongholds.
—2 Corinthians 10:4

Think of your Spirit-directed prayers as "smart bombs" landing on enemy strongholds. Your persevering prayers are precisely and systematically destroying Satan's hold. —*Live a Praying Life*

"Yet a time is coming and has now come when the true worshipers will worship the Father in spirit and truth, for they are the kind of worshipers the Father seeks. God is spirit, and his worshipers must worship in spirit and in truth."
—John 4:23–24

Outward forms of worship were intended to express true, inward worship. The danger is that they will disguise inward emptiness. The Holy Spirit is the guard against empty, surface religion. —*Heart's Cry*

*"Your kingdom come, your will be done
on earth as it is in heaven."*
—Matthew 6:10

This is all one petition. The kingdom of God that Jesus taught and preached about is the rule and reign of God taking direct effect and being presently operative in the circumstances of earth.
—Secrets Jesus Shared

"I no longer call you servants, because a servant does not know his master's business. Instead, I have called you friends, for everything that I learned from my Father I have made known to you."

—John 15:15

_____

_____

_____

_____

_____

_____

_____

_____

_____

_____

_____

_____

_____

_____

_____

_____

_____

_____

_____

*J*esus has pulled you into His inner circle, those to whom He will impart His secrets. A person who is following a doctrine need not listen. There is nothing new to know. The person who is following Christ must be continually listening. —*Heart's Cry*

New Hope® Publishers is a division of WMU®, an international organization that challenges Christian believers to understand and be radically involved in God's mission. For more information about WMU, go to www.wmu.com. More information about New Hope books may be found at www.newhopepublishers.com. New Hope books may be purchased at your local bookstore.

If you've been blessed by this book, we would like to hear your story. The publisher and author welcome your comments and suggestions at: newhopereader@wmu.org.

WORLDCRAFTS℠

You can join other caring people to provide income, improved lives, and hope to artisans in poverty around the world.

Own handmade items produced by people in fair-trade, nonexploitative conditions.

Use WorldCrafts℠ products with your *Live a Praying Life Journal*:

Tab your journal with a
distinctive bookmark.
Leather Bookmark (Burgundy)
H094162 • North Africa

Carry your *Live a Praying Life*
items in an eye-catching tote.
Neesha Tote
H104115 • India

A thought-provoking prayer
reminder, perfect for homes,
offices, or church rooms.
Hand-Carved Praying Hands
W044193 • West Bank

For information about WorldCrafts,
please visit www.WorldCraftsVillage.com or call 1-800-968-7301.

Live a Praying Life
Open Your Life to
God's Power and Provision

DVD Leader Kit
ISBN-10: 1-59669-290-1
ISBN-13: 978-1-59669-290-9

Live a Praying Life
Anniversary Edition
ISBN-10: 1-59669-291-X
ISBN-13: 978-1-59669-291-6

Available in bookstores everywhere.

Journal
A Daily Look at God's Power
*   and Provision*
ISBN-10: 1-59669-289-8
ISBN-13: 978-1-59669-289-3

For information about these books or any New Hope product,
visit www.newhopepublishers.com.

More Books by Jennifer Kennedy Dean

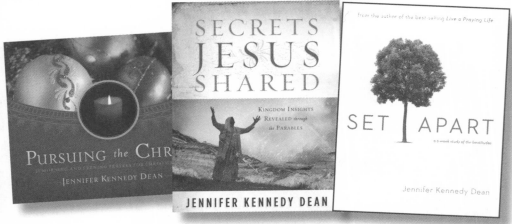

Pursuing the Christ
31 Morning and Evening Prayers
for Christmastime
ISBN-10: 1-59669-231-6
ISBN-13: 978-1-59669-231-2

Secrets Jesus Shared
Kingdom Insights Revealed
Through the Parables
ISBN-10: 1-59669-108-5
ISBN-13: 978-1-59669-108-7

Set Apart
A 6-Week Study
of the Beatitudes
ISBN-10: 1-59669-263-4
ISBN-13: 978-1-59669-263-3

The Life-Changing Power
in the Name of Jesus
ISBN-10: 1-56309-841-5
ISBN-13: 978-1-56309-841-3

Life Unhindered!
Five Keys to Walking in Freedom
ISBN-10: 1-59669-286-3
ISBN-13: 978-1-59669-286-2

Heart's Cry
Principles of Prayer
ISBN-10: 1-59669-095-X
ISBN-13: 978-1-59669-095-0

For information about these books or any New Hope product,
visit www.newhopepublishers.com.
Available in bookstores everywhere.